The
Great Cash Stash

V. Pereira

The Great Cash Stash
Brought To You By The Survivors Of
The Great Depression

ISBN-13: 978-1983659348
ISBN-10: 1983659347

THE GREAT CASH-STASH

THE GREAT CASH-STASH

Dedicated to Jude

THE GREAT CASH-STASH

INDEX

THE GREAT CASH-STASH

PREFACE

Everyone dreams of finding money or treasure and with the economy in a nose dive, there aren't many people out there that couldn't use a few extra dollars in their pockets!

And then, some of us have a fascination with treasure seeking.

Heck, I was just 5 years old when, upon exiting my parents car to have a look-see, I found $20.00 dollars and a ladies watch at a pull off on top of the old Hoover Dam, in Nevada.
Then, in 2004, I was picking up aluminum cans out in the middle of the desert of Arizona on the side of the highway when I found $9600.00! All in $100.00 dollar bills!
And just lately, my family moved into an old adobe house that previously belonged to a man who lived with his mother all his life and then alone after she passed.
Several family members have told me there is probably money hidden somewhere here. They say he had a good job as a carpenter, at a local mining operation until he retired. He was never married, and therefore, had no children, yet there was just enough money in his savings to lay him to rest.
I piddled a little, but have yet to find any money here.
BUT....because if this, I have done a lot of research on the subject so I have decided to share that info with you. That way, whether I find any more money in my lifetime or not, at least all my research might help someone else find some!

The truth is, the last of the survivors of the Great Depression are passing away and leaving the last of the old houses. These old houses have a great potential for hidden cash stashes. That is if the person who lived there was exposed to the great depression or was close to anyone who survived it.

TH E GREAT CASH-STASH

CHAPTER 1

Reasons People hid,
(and sometimes still do hide,) money

Every so often, we hear on the news or through another source, of some lucky guy - or gal, finding a hidden cache of money.
We hear of a house that was being remodeled when, upon smashing through a living room wall, a secret cash of money falls to the floor!
Or of a couple whose dog unearths metal tins of antique gold coins worth millions of dollars!
We wish we could be that lucky.

<u>*And we can, or at least, it is possible.*</u>

Through my years of research, I have found that most hidden money, will have been stashed away by people who survived the Great Depression. And there has never been a better time to find it.

Last but not least, the opportunities are disappearing so now is the best and soon the last times these types of opportunities will be available.

REASON 1:

We'll talk about the Great Depression first.

The Great Depression officially began on October 29th, 1929. This day is historically known as Black Tuesday.

After Black Tuesday, most people who owned stocks began to lose confidence and approximately 16 million shares were sold in one day. The Great Depression had begun and people would indeed suffer for the next ten years.

Many people lost their life savings when banks lost their money. Because of this, people refused to trust banks and began to hide bills, coins, jewelry and more!

Caches have been found in coffee tins, mason jars, ammo boxes, metal and PVC pipes, Sucrets tins, Prince Albert Tins and many other places.

People have accidentally and purposefully found money in thousands of different scenarios. Some of them unimaginable.

REASON 2, 3, 4 and on and on:

Still, there are people that even during these modern times of electronic money, hide money away for many reasons.

People hide 'mad' money, for just in case they get pissed and want to go do something crazy, or- run away!

People hide money for rainy days.

They hide it because it makes them feel good.

They hide it to buy that bad ass Camaro they've been wanting forever...

Then, something happens and they are never able to return the their hidden stash.

You see....this is just the tip of the iceberg.

THE BOTTOM LINE:

The older a house is, the better the chances of someone hiding money in it!

OH, AND ONE LAST THING:

Of course, if you wish to hunt on property that belongs to someone else, it is imperative that you gain permission first. Even if said property seems abandoned, your best bet is to find who ever is in charge and speak to them, requesting permission to detect for artifacts. If necessary, offer them a portion of what you find in exchange for permission to look for hidden treasure on their or their charges property. Or be creative in your offering.

If anyone says no, give them a business card offering to look for lost items, etc., and letting them know that if they change their minds they can give you a call.

It would really suck, if you found a bunch of gold coins and then owner of the property lays claim to them. Without permission, you could lose your entire find, depending on the circumstances.

TH E GREAT CASH-STASH

CHAPTER 2

In the eye of the beholder

There may be 'hidden' treasure right in front of your eyes.

What may seem useless to you, might actually turn out to be worth hundreds, even thousands of dollars. You will need to research some of the items and theories you come across when determining an items value, if any.
If your house belonged to a depression era senior, the odds are good that there is some thing there, hidden (or in plain sight) and of value.
Whether you just inherited your old home, are buying an older house for remodeling or even just hunting on some others property, you should never overlook the potential for 'hidden money'.

You have to keep an ***open mind*** to what 'treasure' you may encounter and where you may find it.

It's been said, that ninety-five percent of the people who hide valuables in their home lived through the Great Depression in the 1920s and '30s.

If your a lover of old homes, chances are that you have most likely been next to, on top of and/or underneath of someones hidden cache of some sort of treasure.

And you didn't even know it!
$$$

This books for you if -

-You recently inherited Granny's pad.

-You live in an older house and are considering doing some remodeling

-You're considering buying an older home that needs remodeling

-You're interested in learning about hidden money!

-You want to FIND hidden money!

The truth is that most of the time, secret caches of money are in places you and I would normally, never think of to look.
That's right, most hidden money is just that: Hidden.
And us humans can be really creative when it comes to hiding things.
And hidden money can be hidden just about anywhere.

Of course, most hidden money is fairly accessible to the person hiding it. But then, not always. Sometimes it is sheet rocked over, inside a brick wall, or buried beneath a lemon tree.

Hidden money can be secreted anywhere.

So do yourself a favor and never **underestimate the hider or limit the finder!**

CHAPTER 3

Before you start your search

You need to prepare your mind, if you want to have the best chance possible, of finding money.
If you know the history of the house, and possibly, even the owners then there are questions you need to ask yourself or the owners about the last owner of the property and about the property itself.

FIRST AND FOREMOST - Most people that hide money like to keep an eye on it. Consider this when deciding where to look, what to tear out, what to pull up, what to knock down.
You can learn a lot by sitting/laying/standing in the previous owners favorite spots.
Did they have a favorite chair or place to sit. Sit there and look around you.
Are there areas of the house outside of the favorite room you are in that you have a plain view of? Check there.
Are there any windows with views? What can you see? Go outside and dig there.
Same for the bedroom. Sit/lay down in their spot in the bedroom and look around.
Check the views from the windows while sitting/laying down.
Many people would hide money in glass, jars, tin cans, ammunition boxes or any other container. So sometimes, using a metal detector can help. Sometimes, not so much.

Did your loved one suffer from Alzheimer's?
How old were they when they got Alzheimer's.
How old were they when they passed.

There may be hidden stashes they forgot about due to Alzheimer's or other health events, that could cause them to not be able to actually retrieve it, but if their memory was still functioning at the time of their death, and/or they were home until the last bits of their lives, most of their stash will be in a place they can actually get to.

Remember to ask yourself questions about the hiding relatives character.
Do you remember your loved one talking about not using banks to save their money or that they didn't trust banks?Were there specific items they told you and others to stay away from OR to be sure not to throw away or let get away from the family?

Were there items that seemed really out of place?
Did they often sneak away to the shed, (or the backyard or anywhere else on their property)?
Did they often mention a specific item they wanted you to have?

FOOTNOTE:
Before you begin your search, as early on as possible, be sure to to start compiling a list of Antique dealers as well as a list of people who are looking to buy certain items.
If you do, over time, the list will become one of the most invaluable tools you'll ever posses.

CHAPTER 4

Look hard for clues

If you hid a thousand dollars somewhere inside or outside your home, would you put it in a spot where you could keep an eye on it?

Yes, you say? Well, I think it's a great idea too, and so did Granny. I don't know about your Granny, but mine had a bunch of money hidden in the corner of her shed, closest to her house and view-able from her bed via her bedroom window. And Granny was no ordinary Granny. In her later days, she went high tech and had a light with a motion sensor hooked up over the padlocked double doors of the shed where her 60 Something Shelby Mustang was kept, which was also view-able from Granny's bed.

How do I know all this? Because Granny had me go out and retrieve it and then re-bury it once, when I lost all the money for the Girl Scout cookies that I had sold.

Good old Granny. They don't make 'em like that any more.

Line of sight prospecting

If you know where Granny's favorite chair was and/or which side of the bed she slept on. If there is a window in front of the sink she can look out while she washes the dishes.

Go to these places and sit/lay/stand. Then look out the windows and any open doors. What does the line of sight lead you to?

If you are looking into another room of the house while sitting/laying/standing in your Grannies favorite spot, you need to look carefully at all woodwork, tiles, brickwork, or anything that might be movable, push-able, pull-able, pried or otherwise manipulated. Also, if there are any mirrors, check all views from mirrors. Granny had a few good ones up her sleeve. And sometimes, she had her mirrors set up where she could see behind her back.

I always wondered why she said she had 'eyes' in the back of her head when she would bust us doin' something we shouldn't have been doing.

Most people who hide cash, like to be able to keep an eye out on it as much as possible. So it's not that surprising to find that when sitting in Granny's chair, you have a perfect view of that little Gnome in front of that old lemon tree.

Search each wall for marks and scratches (pencil, pen, thumbtack..etc...) that seem out of place or odd.

If a room has panel in it, be sure to check for signs where the panel has been or can be pulled away. Especially along joints or in the corners of a room.

 Also consider the the design and decor.
Is there older wallpaper?
Any remodeling during the 1950-1970 era?
Are there any false walls?
Is there any paneling. Whole wall and half.
Is there any brickwork like a fireplace and mantle, brick walls, brick walls in basements.
Is the chimney in service?
Any built in shelves or other units?
Older carpeting like orange or avocado shag?

There could be a million clues or none, but if the house is old enough for people who lived through the depression to have lived in it for any amount of time, there is a good chance there is some hidden stash somewhere within the property boundaries.

CHAPTER 5

A few words about being thorough

Since you will be there to find money or other treasure, you may as well give it your all. One thing you need to be sure to do is to be thorough. I'm talking from drawers in your kitchen to the drawers in your clothes dresser. Be sure to check all the places listed below with a keen eye.
There have been many a clever hider!

DRAWERS

Drawers are a big part of our lives and can be found in a lot of our home furnishings including but not limited to desks, dressers, buffets, china cabinets, under beds, in the kitchen, below a work bench.

When ever I speak of 'drawers' in this book, be aware that you should not only look in the drawers, but you need to take the drawers completely out of their housing.
Depending on the setup, each drawer could be installed in it's own compartment with sides all the way around each individual drawer or it could be just a frame with the hardware to facilitate the drawer for sliding in and out and storing. There are many other configurations.
The point is, that you need to take the drawers out, look on all the sides and the bottom of the drawers for taped envelopes or similar that contains hidden money. Also, check the drawers for a false bottom by measuring the inside height vs. the outside height.
Next, check inside the area where the drawer was. Look for

envelopes or Ziploc baggies taped to the sides and even taped to the top inside compartment that houses the drawers.

BEHIND OLD (and new) PICTURES, PAINTINGS AND OTHER WALL COVERINGS AND ADORNMENTS.

Behind old (and new) pictures and paintings.
Of course, the obvious thing to look for first, would be a safe. At least, that's how it goes in the movies and sometimes in real life.
People sometimes tape money to the back of a hanging picture or painting. Also be sure if there is a back that comes off to take the picture/painting/etc apart and check in between the back of the pic and the back of the frame where it can't be seen.
Be sure to check behind each item that is in the frame if more than one is found.
Also look for any small holes in walls and or woodwork. Some people choose to put a hole or a slit in a wall and just dump coins or bills in whenever they have a chance to do so.
Also, be sure to check the back of any Taxidermy Trophies for any stash spots or hidden compartments.

BEHIND AND INSIDE ALL CHINA CABINETS, HUTCHES, BUFFETTS..ETC.:

Be sure to move all furniture that stands against the wall.
Check the backs, the bottoms and any drawers*.

COUCHES AND OTHER FURNITURE WITH CUSIONS:

In a piece of furniture that has cushions, If the cushions have covers with a zipper, unzip the cover of the cushion and search inside, between the cushion and the inside cover of the couch cushions.

Look under any carpets, rugs, etc. People have installed hidden safes under carpeting. Depression stashes have been found under a loosened floorboard or two underneath carpeting and in rooms with the floorboards in plain view.

Inside pillows with sewn covers. Even bedroom pillows. Most old ladies can sew and will make a small hole in a a pillow, or even a mattress and add money, then sew up the hole.

KITCHEN CABINETS AND ANY OTHER PLACE WITH STORAGE:

Look at the INSIDE of all cabinets and check all interior surfaces, top and bottom for envelopes, Ziploc etc. that may be taped or wedged out of sight.

GARDEN

Underneath and near, Statues and smaller yard markings.
Brick pathways and outdoor fireplaces, look for brick/s that
are lose and see if you can remove it without force. You might find
a small cache behind one.

THE GREAT CASH-STASH

CHAPTER 6

Where to look

There are literally hundreds, if not thousands of places to look for hidden money.
The following is a list to help you get started. Don't stop there, though. When you're through with this list, look around and ask yourself where else might be a good place to hide something. I'm sure you'll think up a few more places to look.

(P.S....At the back of this book, there is a section for you to keep track of your future searches with copies of my checklists that follow. Be sure and check it out!)

______air vents
______floor registers
______underneath all carpets
______false floor panels
______garden
______light fixtures
______loose legs on furniture
______inside piano bench
______figurines (stuffed inside)
______under window sills
______rolled up in socks
______inside books (also check for taped or stashed bills
behind sleeve if book has one.)

______behind medicine cabinet

______check for plumbing for pipes in your pluming that
   might actually be stash spots
______watch for book 'safes' where book is hollowed out in
   middle.
______shoes, be sure to check the toe area

______encyclopedias – check each one for stashed money
   between pages.
______inside speaker cabinets
______inside toilet tank
______taped to bottom of toilet tank
______taped to the underneath sinks
______a hole in the wall covered with a poster.
______a hole in the wall under a stairway.
______taped to the top of a door.
______inside a smoke detector
______in the freezer
______in a box of Tampons (or any container under a sink)
______inside and underneath old sewing machines.

Check for false bottoms in trunks, tool boxes, toy-boxes, tackle boxes, etc., taped to the underneath bottom OR the back of hutches, china cabinets, tall dressers, buffets, etc..beds, mattress. (Especially LOOK INSIDE the mattress. This is one of the most common places depression money was horded and later found.)

Look in their clothes and not just the pockets, they might have sewed something into the hems or virtually anywhere on the garment.

CHAPTER 7

Places that are not so obvious

While some money might be in one of the above, more obvious spots, here is a list of some less obvious places you can check.
One of those little cameras with a bendable attachment for the lense would be a great tool to have for some of the places on the following list.

BE SURE TO CHECK:
-on top of a suspended ceiling
-in attics
-inside of walls
-under false floors
-behind false walls (check closet walls too)
-behind all electrical outlets
-buried stashes in the basement
-bottom of deep freeze
-underneath any runners on stairs, hallways and other places
-refrigerator inside container or Ziploc, even wrapped in white paper or foil like meat. etc.
-behind bricks in basement, floor of basement, old fireplaces.
-inside flower pots, look for Ziploc or other waterproof containers inside the soil.
-envelope/s taped behind the plumbing under sinks and behind toilets
-stitched into hems of curtains, jackets, other sew-able items
-in abandoned piping or piping that looks connected but isn't actually connected and is fairly easily accessible.

-pipes with caps on them, including piping accessible in basement.
-in the kitchen (food containers/freezer/fridge)
-underneath installed carpet

CHAPTER 8

Outside

Imagine – you're outside in your yard with your dog when it begins to dig furiously at something. You wonder what the excitement is about so you go over to see what the dog is digging up. Upon inspection, you realize 'Fido' just hit the jackpot! Your dog just dug up a rusted out coffee can filled to its rusted out brim, with what looks like solid gold coins that turn out to be worth millions of dollars!

That's what happened to a California couple in the not so distant past. And they weren't even looking for hidden or lost treasure. Just taking the dog out for a walk.

If only it were always that easy, but then again, if it was, would there be any hidden or lost money for us to look for?

Lots of hidden money has been found outside of the house.
As a matter of fact, lots of folks that hid money inside, hid money outside. Some say it was just in case the house burned, they would still have money put away.
Also, lots of folks hid money outside only. So keep that in mind if you don't find any cash-stashes in the house that the possibility is that your treasure is still within reach.

Many people would hide money by a certain tree. Many times, they would use a marker, like the little ceramic elf I mentioned at the beginning of the book.

Also, if there is a sidewalk, or concrete foundation for a shed, people would dig a stash spot right below the edge of the concrete and hide money there.

Sheds and all other outbuildings.
Search all cars on property thoroughly
Search all boxes, cans, containers in all out buildings.
Inside corners of any dirt floors
Check under the base/foot of hollowed out doors
Check out all removable top cans--paint, chemicals
Don't forget the doghouse and under the doghouse in the back yard
Chicken Coops too.

Water Wells.
  Look for loose bricks all the way down to arms length.
  Also look for loose bricks around the outside of the fireplace.

   Look for depressions in the ground around and behind the house, all other buildings and the entire yard. If it sits on acreage, you need to go over every inch of that land looking for depressions and other hiding spots. I would use a metal detector there as well.

   If there was an outhouse in the old days, it can't hurt to find out it's location and dig there. You will surely find some old bottles and maybe some old money.

CHAPTER 9

Other places to look for lost money
(Depression and non-depression)

Not all hidden money is depression money. And not all found money is hidden money.

Lost money deserves a chapter here in this book about finding hidden money.

If you're out on a road trip and are bored, or broke...be sure to check any and all pull offs on the side of any street, highway, road, etc., that is used often by passers by to get out of the car and stretch, relieve their bladders, drink a beer or see a sight.

When people are riding in or driving a car, they come up with all kinds of spots to stick that change they just got at a drive through, or the twenty a friend owed and just threw into their window as they are leaving work.

You know. Situations where money gets set under your leg, or on your lap or on the dash when your in your car.

Lots of people get out of their cars and lose money. It happens all the time.

At the gas station.
At the store.
At the little league game.

Scan all parking lots when out. Especially convenience stores.

Most of all, get out to search the edges of any weedy areas as, if paper money is lost as soon as the wind blows, this is where it will end up.

# THE GREAT CASH-STASH

CHAPTER 10

When all else fails

Sometimes, even with the most ambitious hunts, treasure will not be found.

Sometimes it's because ***there is no treasure.***

Other times, it's because you ***just haven't found*** the ***right place.***

While some treasure seekers will have already given up, there are those of us who are still looking.
If you're still reading this, then you are probably the kind who will still be looking and that's great!
Us adults are often, so easily side-tracked by preconceived notions, (from years of being human) that we overlook things a twelve year old would not be able to ignore.
That being said, if you have any clever tween nephews or nieces it would be a smart move to recruit two or three of them to hunt for treasure at your site. Offer them a part of the pay.
Once there, tell them of the possibilities of treasure but don't tell them where to look, or where not to look.
They will come up with places you never dreamed of looking since they have no preconceived ideas about were a person might hide money.
Not to mention, they can get into and crawl through places *you wouldn't, maybe even couldn't crawl through.*

CHAPTER 11

Whatever you do, don't give up.

There are so many places where people have hidden money that I barely touched the tip of the iceberg here with this book.
Hopefully, it's enough to get you started and even more, to help you find something good!
Keep in mind, as the old saying goes, "If at first you don't succeed, try, try, again".
It's when it seems like you'll never find a thing that you are probably at your closest to finding something so what ever you do, don't give up easily. Perseverance pays off when searching for hidden money, so plan on bringing a good helping of it when you head out to a new search.
If you get frustrated, take a break and then go back to try again. Just don't give up!

Here's a few more ideas if you are about to give up....

If you happen to know a cop or even a friend with a search dog, offer them part of anything found to bring their search dog to search the house and yard. Have them mark the places the dog hits on.

If you're into it, hire a psychic to help you find that hidden treasure.

Go online and search GOOGLE for 'hidden money' and see if you can find inspiration there. Google the images for the term 'hidden money'. Maybe something there can inspire you find that treasure.

TH E GREAT CASH-STASH

CHAPTER 12

Examples

A friend of mines Aunt used to roll up money and put it into beer and soda bottles, then she "Threw it away' at the dump on the old ranch where she lived. When she died, over $18,000.00 dollars was found in bottles through-out the permanent dump.

Another friend of mine told me that when his Granny passed, he found an old Mexican Coffee tin, buried two feet from the back door. It was approximately 18 inches deep.
The family was pleasantly surprised when they found the tin contained 1500 Silver dollars dated from the turn of the century up to the 1920's.

And yet, another friend's Nana hid money directly under the carpet above the floor boards. $1600.00 in $100 dollar bills were found when she looked under her Nana's carpet!

I had another friend that had a floor safe installed with the lid being a section that fit right in the tongue and grove that covered the floor. I never would have known it was there (and it was in plain view, out in the open) if they hadn't shown me.

TH E GREAT CASH-STASH

PROLOUGE

In the end, I am sure there are a million and one places that I didn't mention in this book. That's because I haven't learned of them yet. I will update this book from time to time to add new places that I hear of or that you, my reader, are kind enough to let me know of.

The best way to do that is to post any new spots, ideas, etc... on my "FIND THAT CASH STASH' Facebook page located at:

https://www.facebook.com/groups/1851878035141927/

So remember, ***just because it's not listed here doesn't mean it's not a good place to look!***

If you can imagine it, someone else might have imagined it too! Any idea is a good one! Keep looking and NEVER, EVER GIVE UP!

Following this, you'll find 'My Searches' logs for multiple searches, including a checklist for each search. I included these to help you keep track.

With that, I'd like to wish you.....

Good Luck and Happy Hunting!

MY SEARCHES

DATE:_______________________________________

ADDRESS:___________________________________

CITY_____________________________STATE_________

WHAT DREW YOU TO THIS PLACE: __________

____

____

____

____

WHAT DID YOU FIND:

____

____

____

____

____

____

CHECK LIST
______air vents
______floor registers
______underneath all carpets
______false floor panels
______garden
______light fixtures
______loose legs on furniture
______inside piano bench
______figurines (stuffed inside)
______under window sills
______rolled up in socks
______inside books (also check for taped or stashed bills
______behind sleeve if book has one.)
______watch for book 'safes' where book is hollowed out in
   middle.
______shoes, be sure to check the toe area
______inside Speaker Cabinets
______inside toilet tank
______taped to bottom of toilet tank
______taped to the underneath sinks
______a hole in the wall covered with a poster.
______a hole in the wall under a stairway.
______taped to the top of a door.
______inside a smoke detector
______in the freezer
______in a box of Tampons (or any container under a sink)
______inside and underneath old sewing machines.
______check for false bottoms in trunks, tool boxes, toy-
   boxes, tackle boxes, etc.
______taped to the underneath bottom OR the back of
   hutches, china cabinets, tall dressers, buffets, etc..
______beds, mattress (Especially INSIDE the mattress.
   This is one of the most common places depression
   money was horded and later found.)
______look in their clothes and not just the pockets, they
   might have sewed something into the hems or virtually
   anywhere on the garment.
______on top of a suspended ceiling

______in attics
______inside of walls
______under false floors
______behind false walls (check closet walls too)
______behind all electrical outlets

______bottom of deep freeze
______underneath any runners on stairs, hallways and other places
______refrigerator inside container or Ziploc, even wrapped in white paper or foil like meat. etc.
______behind bricks in basement, floor of basement, old fireplaces.
______inside flower pots, look for Ziploc or other waterproof containers inside the soil.
______envelope taped behind the plumbing under sinks and behind toilets
______stitched into hems of curtains, jackets, other sew-able items
______in abandoned piping or piping that looks connected but isn't actually connected and is fairly easily accessible. Pipes with caps on them, including piping accessible in basement.
______in the kitchen (food containers/freezer/fridge)
______sheds and all other outbuildings.
______search all cars on property thoroughly
______search all boxes, cans, containers in all out buildings.
______inside corners of any dirt floors
______check under the base/foot of hollowed out doors
______check out all removable top cans--paint, chemicals
______don't forget the doghouse and under-neath the doghouse in the back yard
______chicken coops too.
______check all water wells
______look for loose bricks all the way down to arms length.
______also look for loose bricks around the outside of the fireplace.
______look for depressions in the ground and detect them.

MY SEARCHES

DATE:_______________________________________

ADDRESS:_____________________________________

CITY_____________________________STATE_________

WHAT DREW YOU TO THIS PLACE: __________

____

____

____

____

WHAT DID YOU FIND: ______________________

____

____

____

____

____

____

____

NOTES: _______________________________

____

____

____

____

____

____

____

____

COMMENTS: _______________________________

____

____

____

____

____

____

____

CHECK LIST
_______air vents
_______floor registers
_______underneath all carpets
_______false floor panels
_______garden
_______light fixtures
_______loose legs on furniture
_______inside piano bench
_______figurines (stuffed inside)
_______under window sills
_______rolled up in socks
_______inside books (also check for taped or stashed bills
_______behind sleeve if book has one.)
_______watch for book 'safes' where book is hollowed out in
    middle.
_______shoes, be sure to check the toe area
_______inside Speaker Cabinets
_______inside toilet tank
_______taped to bottom of toilet tank
_______taped to the underneath sinks
_______a hole in the wall covered with a poster.
_______a hole in the wall under a stairway.
_______taped to the top of a door.
_______inside a smoke detector
_______in the freezer
_______in a box of Tampons (or any container under a sink)
_______inside and underneath old sewing machines.
_______check for false bottoms in trunks, tool boxes, toy-
    boxes, tackle boxes, etc.
_______taped to the underneath bottom OR the back of
    hutches, china cabinets, tall dressers, buffets, etc..
_______beds, mattress (Especially INSIDE the mattress.
    This is one of the most common places depression
    money was horded and later found.)
_______look in their clothes and not just the pockets, they
    might have sewed something into the hems or virtually
    anywhere on the garment.
_______on top of a suspended ceiling

______in attics

______inside of walls

______under false floors

______behind false walls (check closet walls too)

______behind all electrical outlets

______bottom of deep freeze

______underneath any runners on stairs, hallways and other places

______refrigerator inside container or Ziploc, even wrapped in white paper or foil like meat. etc.

______behind bricks in basement, floor of basement, old fireplaces.

______inside flower pots, look for Ziploc or other waterproof containers inside the soil.

______envelope taped behind the plumbing under sinks and behind toilets

______stitched into hems of curtains, jackets, other sew-able items

______in abandoned piping or piping that looks connected but isn't actually connected and is fairly easily accessible. Pipes with caps on them, including piping accessible in basement.

______in the kitchen (food containers/freezer/fridge)

______sheds and all other outbuildings.

______search all cars on property thoroughly

______search all boxes, cans, containers in all out buildings.

______inside corners of any dirt floors

______check under the base/foot of hollowed out doors

______check out all removable top cans--paint, chemicals

______don't forget the doghouse and under-neath the doghouse in the back yard

______chicken coops too.

______check all water wells

______look for loose bricks all the way down to arms length.

______also look for loose bricks around the outside of the fireplace.

______look for depressions in the ground around and behind buildings and detect them.

MY SEARCHES

DATE:_______________________________________

ADDRESS:___________________________________

CITY______________________________STATE________

WHAT DREW YOU TO THIS PLACE: __________

____

____

____

____

WHAT DID YOU FIND: ___________________

____

____

____

____

____

____

____

NOTES: _______________________________

____

____

____

____

____

____

____

____

COMMENTS: _______________________________

____

____

____

____

____

____

CHECK LIST

______air vents

______floor registers

______underneath all carpets

______false floor panels

______garden

______light fixtures

______loose legs on furniture

______inside piano bench

______figurines (stuffed inside)

______under window sills

______rolled up in socks

______inside books (also check for taped or stashed bills behind sleeve if book has one.)

______watch for book 'safes' where book is hollowed out in middle.

______shoes, be sure to check the toe area

______inside Speaker Cabinets

______inside toilet tank

______taped to bottom of toilet tank

______taped to the underneath sinks

______a hole in the wall covered with a poster.

______a hole in the wall under a stairway.

______taped to the top of a door.

______inside a smoke detector

______in the freezer

______in a box of Tampons (or any container under a sink)

______inside and underneath old sewing machines.

______check for false bottoms in trunks, tool boxes, toy-boxes, tackle boxes, etc.

______taped to the underneath bottom OR the back of hutches, china cabinets, tall dressers, buffets, etc..

______beds, mattress (Especially INSIDE the mattress. This is one of the most common places depression money was horded and later found.)

______look in their clothes and not just the pockets, they might have sewed something into the hems or virtually anywhere on the garment.

______on top of a suspended ceiling

_______ in attics

_______ inside of walls

_______ under false floors

_______ behind false walls (check closet walls too)

_______ behind all electrical outlets

_______ bottom of deep freeze

_______ underneath any runners on stairs, hallways and other places

_______ refrigerator inside container or Ziploc, even wrapped in white paper or foil like meat. etc.

_______ behind bricks in basement, floor of basement, old fireplaces.

_______ inside flower pots, look for Ziploc or other waterproof containers inside the soil.

_______ envelope taped behind the plumbing under sinks and behind toilets

_______ stitched into hems of curtains, jackets, other sew-able items

_______ in abandoned piping or piping that looks connected but isn't actually connected and is fairly easily accessible. Pipes with caps on them, including piping accessible in basement.

_______ in the kitchen (food containers/freezer/fridge)

_______ sheds and all other outbuildings.

_______ search all cars on property thoroughly

_______ search all boxes, cans, containers in all out buildings.

_______ inside corners of any dirt floors

_______ check under the base/foot of hollowed out doors

_______ check out all removable top cans--paint, chemicals

_______ don't forget the doghouse and under-neath the doghouse in the back yard

_______ chicken coops too.

_______ check all water wells

_______ look for loose bricks all the way down to arms length.

_______ also look for loose bricks around the outside of the fireplace.

_______ look for depressions in the ground around and behind buildings and detect them.

MY SEARCHES

DATE:___________________________________

ADDRESS:_______________________________

CITY___________________________STATE________

WHAT DREW YOU TO THIS PLACE: __________

____

____

____

____

WHAT DID YOU FIND: ____________________

____

____

____

____

____

____

____

NOTES: ______________________________

____

____

____

____

____

____

____

____

____

COMMENTS: ______________________________

____

____

____

____

____

____

CHECK LIST

______air vents

______floor registers

______underneath all carpets

______false floor panels

______garden

______light fixtures

______loose legs on furniture

______inside piano bench

______figurines (stuffed inside)

______under window sills

______rolled up in socks

______inside books (also check for taped or stashed bills behind sleeve if book has one.)

______watch for book 'safes' where book is hollowed out in middle.

______shoes, be sure to check the toe area

______inside Speaker Cabinets

______inside toilet tank

______taped to bottom of toilet tank

______taped to the underneath sinks

______a hole in the wall covered with a poster.

______a hole in the wall under a stairway.

______taped to the top of a door.

______inside a smoke detector

______in the freezer

______in a box of Tampons (or any container under a sink)

______inside and underneath old sewing machines.

______check for false bottoms in trunks, tool boxes, toy-boxes, tackle boxes, etc.

______taped to the underneath bottom OR the back of hutches, china cabinets, tall dressers, buffets, etc..

______beds, mattress (Especially INSIDE the mattress. This is one of the most common places depression money was horded and later found.)

______look in their clothes and not just the pockets, they might have sewed something into the hems or virtually anywhere on the garment.

______on top of a suspended ceiling

______in attics
______inside of walls
______under false floors
______behind false walls (check closet walls too)
______behind all electrical outlets
______bottom of deep freeze
______underneath any runners on stairs, hallways and other places
______refrigerator inside container or Ziploc, even wrapped in white paper or foil like meat. etc.
______behind bricks in basement, floor of basement, old fireplaces.
______inside flower pots, look for Ziploc or other waterproof containers inside the soil.
______envelope taped behind the plumbing under sinks and behind toilets
______stitched into hems of curtains, jackets, other sew-able items
______in abandoned piping or piping that looks connected but isn't actually connected and is fairly easily accessible. Pipes with caps on them, including piping accessible in basement.
______in the kitchen (food containers/freezer/fridge)
______sheds and all other outbuildings.
______search all cars on property thoroughly
______search all boxes, cans, containers in all out buildings.
______inside corners of any dirt floors
______check under the base/foot of hollowed out doors
______check out all removable top cans--paint, chemicals
______don't forget the doghouse and under-neath the doghouse in the back yard
______chicken coops too.
______check all water wells
______look for loose bricks all the way down to arms length.
______also look for loose bricks around the outside of the fireplace.
______look for depressions in the ground around and behind buildings and detect them.

MY SEARCHES

DATE:_______________________________________

ADDRESS:_________________________________

CITY______________________________STATE________

WHAT DREW YOU TO THIS PLACE: __________

____

____

____

____

WHAT DID YOU FIND: ____________________

____

____

____

____

____

____

____

NOTES: _______________________

COMMENTS: _______________________

CHECK LIST

______air vents
______floor registers
______underneath all carpets
______false floor panels
______garden
______light fixtures
______loose legs on furniture
______inside piano bench
______figurines (stuffed inside)
______under window sills
______rolled up in socks
______inside books (also check for taped or stashed bills
______behind sleeve if book has one.)
______watch for book 'safes' where book is hollowed out in
 middle.
______shoes, be sure to check the toe area
______inside Speaker Cabinets
______inside toilet tank
______taped to bottom of toilet tank
______taped to the underneath sinks
______a hole in the wall covered with a poster.
______a hole in the wall under a stairway.
______taped to the top of a door.
______inside a smoke detector
______in the freezer
______in a box of Tampons (or any container under a sink)
______inside and underneath old sewing machines.
______check for false bottoms in trunks, tool boxes, toy-
 boxes, tackle boxes, etc.
______taped to the underneath bottom OR the back of
 hutches, china cabinets, tall dressers, buffets, etc..
______beds, mattress (Especially INSIDE the mattress.
 This is one of the most common places depression
 money was horded and later found.)
______look in their clothes and not just the pockets, they
 might have sewed something into the hems or virtually
 anywhere on the garment.
______on top of a suspended ceiling

THE GREAT CASH-STASH

______in attics

______inside of walls

______under false floors

______behind false walls (check closet walls too)

______behind all electrical outlets

______bottom of deep freeze

______underneath any runners on stairs, hallways and other places

______refrigerator inside container or Ziploc, even wrapped in white paper or foil like meat. etc.

______behind bricks in basement, floor of basement, old fireplaces.

______inside flower pots, look for Ziploc or other waterproof containers inside the soil.

______envelope taped behind the plumbing under sinks and behind toilets

______stitched into hems of curtains, jackets, other sew-able items

______in abandoned piping or piping that looks connected but isn't actually connected and is fairly easily accessible. Pipes with caps on them, including piping accessible in basement.

______in the kitchen (food containers/freezer/fridge)

______sheds and all other outbuildings.

______search all cars on property thoroughly

______search all boxes, cans, containers in all out buildings.

______inside corners of any dirt floors

______check under the base/foot of hollowed out doors

______check out all removable top cans--paint, chemicals

______don't forget the doghouse and under-neath the doghouse in the back yard

______chicken coops too.

______check all water wells

______look for loose bricks all the way down to arms length.

______also look for loose bricks around the outside of the fireplace.

______look for depressions in the ground around and behind buildings and detect them.

MY SEARCHES

DATE:_______________________________________

ADDRESS:_____________________________________

CITY_______________________STATE_________

WHAT DREW YOU TO THIS PLACE: __________

____

____

____

____

WHAT DID YOU FIND: ___________________

____

____

____

____

____

____

____

NOTES: _______________________

____

____

____

____

____

____

____

____

____

COMMENTS: _______________________

____

____

____

____

____

____

____

CHECK LIST
______air vents
______floor registers
______underneath all carpets
______false floor panels
______garden
______light fixtures
______loose legs on furniture
______inside piano bench
______figurines (stuffed inside)
______under window sills
______rolled up in socks
______inside books (also check for taped or stashed bills
______behind sleeve if book has one.)
______watch for book 'safes' where book is hollowed out in
   middle.
______shoes, be sure to check the toe area
______inside Speaker Cabinets
______inside toilet tank
______taped to bottom of toilet tank
______taped to the underneath sinks
______a hole in the wall covered with a poster.
______a hole in the wall under a stairway.
______taped to the top of a door.
______inside a smoke detector
______in the freezer
______in a box of Tampons (or any container under a sink)
______inside and underneath old sewing machines.
______check for false bottoms in trunks, tool boxes, toy-
   boxes, tackle boxes, etc.
______taped to the underneath bottom OR the back of
   hutches, china cabinets, tall dressers, buffets, etc..
   beds, mattress (Especially INSIDE the mattress.
   This is one of the most common places depression
   money was horded and later found.)
______look in their clothes and not just the pockets, they
   might have sewed something into the hems or virtually
   anywhere on the garment.
______on top of a suspended ceiling

______in attics
______inside of walls
______under false floors
______behind false walls (check closet walls too)
______behind all electrical outlets
______bottom of deep freeze
______underneath any runners on stairs, hallways and other places
______refrigerator inside container or Ziploc, even wrapped in white paper or foil like meat. etc.
______behind bricks in basement, floor of basement, old fireplaces.
______inside flower pots, look for Ziploc or other waterproof containers inside the soil.
______envelope taped behind the plumbing under sinks and behind toilets
______stitched into hems of curtains, jackets, other sew-able items
______in abandoned piping or piping that looks connected but isn't actually connected and is fairly easily accessible. Pipes with caps on them, including piping accessible in basement.
______in the kitchen (food containers/freezer/fridge)
______sheds and all other outbuildings.
______search all cars on property thoroughly
______search all boxes, cans, containers in all out buildings.
______inside corners of any dirt floors
______check under the base/foot of hollowed out doors
______check out all removable top cans--paint, chemicals
______don't forget the doghouse and under-neath the doghouse in the back yard
______chicken coops too.
______check all water wells
______look for loose bricks all the way down to arms length.
______also look for loose bricks around the outside of the fireplace.
______look for depressions in the ground around and behind buildings and detect them.

MY SEARCHES

DATE:_______________________________________

ADDRESS:_____________________________________

CITY_____________________________STATE________

WHAT DREW YOU TO THIS PLACE: __________

____

____

____

____

WHAT DID YOU FIND: _______________________

____

____

____

____

____

____

____

NOTES: ______________________________

____

____

____

____

____

____

____

____

COMMENTS: ______________________________

____

____

____

____

____

____

____

CHECK LIST
______air vents
______floor registers
______underneath all carpets
______false floor panels
______garden
______light fixtures
______loose legs on furniture
______inside piano bench
______figurines (stuffed inside)
______under window sills
______rolled up in socks
______inside books (also check for taped or stashed bills
______behind sleeve if book has one.)
______watch for book 'safes' where book is hollowed out in
    middle.
______shoes, be sure to check the toe area
______inside Speaker Cabinets
______inside toilet tank
______taped to bottom of toilet tank
______taped to the underneath sinks
______a hole in the wall covered with a poster.
______a hole in the wall under a stairway.
______taped to the top of a door.
______inside a smoke detector
______in the freezer
______in a box of Tampons (or any container under a sink)
______inside and underneath old sewing machines.
______check for false bottoms in trunks, tool boxes, toy-
    boxes, tackle boxes, etc.
______taped to the underneath bottom OR the back of
    hutches, china cabinets, tall dressers, buffets, etc..
______beds, mattress (Especially INSIDE the mattress.
    This is one of the most common places depression
    money was horded and later found.)
______look in their clothes and not just the pockets, they
    might have sewed something into the hems or virtually
    anywhere on the garment.
______on top of a suspended ceiling

TH E GREAT CASH-STASH

______in attics

______inside of walls

______under false floors

______behind false walls (check closet walls too)

______behind all electrical outlets

______bottom of deep freeze

______underneath any runners on stairs, hallways and other places

______refrigerator inside container or Ziploc, even wrapped in white paper or foil like meat. etc.

______behind bricks in basement, floor of basement, old fireplaces.

______inside flower pots, look for Ziploc or other waterproof containers inside the soil.

______envelope taped behind the plumbing under sinks and behind toilets

______stitched into hems of curtains, jackets, other sew-able items

______in abandoned piping or piping that looks connected but isn't actually connected and is fairly easily accessible. Pipes with caps on them, including piping accessible in basement.

______in the kitchen (food containers/freezer/fridge)

______sheds and all other outbuildings.

______search all cars on property thoroughly

______search all boxes, cans, containers in all out buildings.

______inside corners of any dirt floors

______check under the base/foot of hollowed out doors

______check out all removable top cans--paint, chemicals

______don't forget the doghouse and under-neath the doghouse in the back yard

______chicken coops too.

______check all water wells

______look for loose bricks all the way down to arms length.

______also look for loose bricks around the outside of the fireplace.

______look for depressions in the ground around and behind buildings and detect them.

MY SEARCHES

DATE:____

ADDRESS:____________________________________

CITY____________________________STATE________

WHAT DREW YOU TO THIS PLACE: ___________

____

____

____

____

WHAT DID YOU FIND: _____________________

____

____

____

____

____

____

____

____

NOTES: _______________________________

____

____

____

____

____

____

____

____

COMMENTS: _______________________________

____

____

____

____

____

____

____

CHECK LIST

_____air vents
_____floor registers
_____underneath all carpets
_____false floor panels
_____garden
_____light fixtures
_____loose legs on furniture
_____inside piano bench
_____figurines (stuffed inside)
_____under window sills
_____rolled up in socks
_____inside books (also check for taped or stashed bills
_____behind sleeve if book has one.)
_____watch for book 'safes' where book is hollowed out in
  middle.
_____shoes, be sure to check the toe area
_____inside Speaker Cabinets
_____inside toilet tank
_____taped to bottom of toilet tank
_____taped to the underneath sinks
_____a hole in the wall covered with a poster.
_____a hole in the wall under a stairway.
_____taped to the top of a door.
_____inside a smoke detector
_____in the freezer
_____in a box of Tampons (or any container under a sink)
_____inside and underneath old sewing machines.
_____check for false bottoms in trunks, tool boxes, toy-
  boxes, tackle boxes, etc.
_____taped to the underneath bottom OR the back of
  hutches, china cabinets, tall dressers, buffets, etc..
_____beds, mattress (Especially INSIDE the mattress.
  This is one of the most common places depression
  money was horded and later found.)
_____look in their clothes and not just the pockets, they
  might have sewed something into the hems or virtually
  anywhere on the garment.
_____on top of a suspended ceiling

______ in attics

______ inside of walls

______ under false floors

______ behind false walls (check closet walls too)

______ behind all electrical outlets

______ bottom of deep freeze

______ underneath any runners on stairs, hallways and other places

______ refrigerator inside container or Ziploc, even wrapped in white paper or foil like meat. etc.

______ behind bricks in basement, floor of basement, old fireplaces.

______ inside flower pots, look for Ziploc or other waterproof containers inside the soil.

______ envelope taped behind the plumbing under sinks and behind toilets

______ stitched into hems of curtains, jackets, other sew-able items

______ in abandoned piping or piping that looks connected but isn't actually connected and is fairly easily accessible. Pipes with caps on them, including piping accessible in basement.

______ in the kitchen (food containers/freezer/fridge)

______ sheds and all other outbuildings.

______ search all cars on property thoroughly

______ search all boxes, cans, containers in all out buildings.

______ inside corners of any dirt floors

______ check under the base/foot of hollowed out doors

______ check out all removable top cans--paint, chemicals

______ don't forget the doghouse and under-neath the doghouse in the back yard

______ chicken coops too.

______ check all water wells

______ look for loose bricks all the way down to arms length.

______ also look for loose bricks around the outside of the fireplace.

______ look for depressions in the ground around and behind buildings and detect them.

MY SEARCHES

DATE:_______________________________________

ADDRESS:_______________________________________

CITY____________________________STATE__________

WHAT DREW YOU TO THIS PLACE: __________

____

____

____

____

WHAT DID YOU FIND: _______________________

____

____

____

____

____

____

____

____

NOTES: _______________________

____

____

____

____

____

____

____

COMMENTS: _______________________

____

____

____

____

____

____

CHECK LIST
______air vents
______floor registers
______underneath all carpets
______false floor panels
______garden
______light fixtures
______loose legs on furniture
______inside piano bench
______figurines (stuffed inside)
______under window sills
______rolled up in socks
______inside books (also check for taped or stashed bills
______behind sleeve if book has one.)
______watch for book 'safes' where book is hollowed out in
   middle.
______shoes, be sure to check the toe area
______inside speaker cabinets
______inside toilet tank
______taped to bottom of toilet tank
______taped to the underneath sinks
______a hole in the wall covered with a poster.
______a hole in the wall under a stairway.
______taped to the top of a door.
______inside a smoke detector
______in the freezer
______in a box of Tampons (or any container under a sink)
______inside and underneath old sewing machines.
______check for false bottoms in trunks, tool boxes, toy-
   boxes, tackle boxes, etc.
______taped to the underneath bottom OR the back of
   hutches, china cabinets, tall dressers, buffets, etc..
______beds, mattress (Especially INSIDE the mattress.
   This is one of the most common places depression
   money was horded and later found.)
______look in their clothes and not just the pockets, they
   might have sewed something into the hems or virtually
   anywhere on the garment.
______on top of a suspended ceiling

______in attics
______inside of walls
______under false floors
______behind false walls (check closet walls too)
______behind all electrical outlets
______bottom of deep freeze
______underneath any runners on stairs, hallways and other
places
______refrigerator inside container or Ziploc, even wrapped
in white paper or foil like meat. etc.
______behind bricks in basement, floor of basement, old
fireplaces.
______inside flower pots, look for Ziploc or other
waterproof containers inside the soil.
______envelope taped behind the plumbing under sinks and
behind toilets
______stitched into hems of curtains, jackets, other sew-able
 items
______in abandoned piping or piping that looks connected
but isn't actually connected and is fairly easily
accessible. Pipes with caps on them, including piping
accessible in basement.
______in the kitchen (food containers/freezer/fridge)
______sheds and all other outbuildings.
______search all cars on property thoroughly
______search all boxes, cans, containers in all out buildings.
______inside corners of any dirt floors
______check under the base/foot of hollowed out doors
______check out all removable top cans--paint, chemicals
______don't forget the doghouse and under-neath the
doghouse in the back yard
______chicken coops too.
______check all water wells
______look for loose bricks all the way down to arms
length.
______also look for loose bricks around the outside of the
fireplace.
______look for depressions in the ground around and
behind buildings and detect them.

MY SEARCHES

DATE:_______________________________________

75

ADDRESS:_____________________________________

CITY__________________________STATE_________

WHAT DREW YOU TO THIS PLACE: __________

____

____

____

WHAT DID YOU FIND: _____________________

____

____

____

____

____

____

____

NOTES: __________________________

____

____

____

____

____

____

____

____

COMMENTS: __________________________

____

____

____

____

____

____

CHECK LIST
______air vents
______floor registers
______underneath all carpets
______false floor panels
______garden
______light fixtures
______loose legs on furniture
______inside piano bench
______figurines (stuffed inside)
______under window sills
______rolled up in socks
______inside books (also check for taped or stashed bills
______behind sleeve if book has one.)
______watch for book 'safes' where book is hollowed out in
      middle.
______shoes, be sure to check the toe area
______inside Speaker Cabinets
______inside toilet tank
______taped to bottom of toilet tank
______taped to the underneath sinks
______a hole in the wall covered with a poster.
______a hole in the wall under a stairway.
______taped to the top of a door.
______inside a smoke detector
______in the freezer
______in a box of Tampons (or any container under a sink)
______inside and underneath old sewing machines.
______check for false bottoms in trunks, tool boxes, toy-
      boxes, tackle boxes, etc.
______taped to the underneath bottom OR the back of
      hutches, china cabinets, tall dressers, buffets, etc..
______beds, mattress (Especially INSIDE the mattress.
      This is one of the most common places depression
      money was horded and later found.)
______look in their clothes and not just the pockets, they
      might have sewed something into the hems or virtually
      anywhere on the garment.
______on top of a suspended ceiling

TH E GREAT CASH-STASH

_______in attics
_______inside of walls
_______under false floors
_______behind false walls (check closet walls too)
_______behind all electrical outlets
_______bottom of deep freeze
_______underneath any runners on stairs, hallways and other places
_______refrigerator inside container or Ziploc, even wrapped in white paper or foil like meat. etc.
_______behind bricks in basement, floor of basement, old fireplaces.
_______inside flower pots, look for Ziploc or other waterproof containers inside the soil.
_______envelope taped behind the plumbing under sinks and behind toilets
_______stitched into hems of curtains, jackets, other sew-able items
_______in abandoned piping or piping that looks connected but isn't actually connected and is fairly easily accessible. Pipes with caps on them, including piping accessible in basement.
_______in the kitchen (food containers/freezer/fridge)
_______sheds and all other outbuildings.
_______search all cars on property thoroughly
_______search all boxes, cans, containers in all out buildings.
_______inside corners of any dirt floors
_______check under the base/foot of hollowed out doors
_______check out all removable top cans--paint, chemicals
_______don't forget the doghouse and under-neath the doghouse in the back yard
_______chicken coops too
_______check all water wells
_______look for loose bricks all the way down to arms length.
_______also look for loose bricks around the outside of the fireplace.
_______look for depressions in the ground around and behind buildings and detect them.

MY SEARCHES

DATE:_______________________________________

ADDRESS:_________________________________

CITY_____________________________STATE_________

WHAT DREW YOU TO THIS PLACE: __________

____

____

____

____

WHAT DID YOU FIND: _____________________

____

____

____

____

____

____

____

NOTES: ____________________________

____

____

____

____

____

____

____

____

COMMENTS: ____________________________

____

____

____

____

____

____

CHECK LIST
______air vents
______floor registers
______underneath all carpets
______false floor panels
______garden
______light fixtures
______loose legs on furniture
______inside piano bench
______figurines (stuffed inside)
______under window sills
______rolled up in socks
______inside books (also check for taped or stashed bills
______behind sleeve if book has one.)
______watch for book 'safes' where book is hollowed out in
   middle.
______shoes, be sure to check the toe area
______inside Speaker Cabinets
______inside toilet tank
______taped to bottom of toilet tank
______taped to the underneath sinks
______a hole in the wall covered with a poster.
______a hole in the wall under a stairway.
______taped to the top of a door.
______inside a smoke detector
______in the freezer
______in a box of Tampons (or any container under a sink)
______inside and underneath old sewing machines.
______check for false bottoms in trunks, tool boxes, toy-
   boxes, tackle boxes, etc.
______taped to the underneath bottom OR the back of
   hutches, china cabinets, tall dressers, buffets, etc..
______beds, mattress (Especially INSIDE the mattress.
   This is one of the most common places depression
   money was horded and later found.)
______look in their clothes and not just the pockets, they
   might have sewed something into the hems or virtually
   anywhere on the garment.
______on top of a suspended ceiling

______in attics

______inside of walls

______under false floors

______behind false walls (check closet walls too)

______behind all electrical outlets

______bottom of deep freeze

______underneath any runners on stairs, hallways and other places

______refrigerator inside container or Ziploc, even wrapped in white paper or foil like meat. etc.

______behind bricks in basement, floor of basement, old fireplaces.

______inside flower pots, look for Ziploc or other waterproof containers inside the soil.

______envelope taped behind the plumbing under sinks and behind toilets

______stitched into hems of curtains, jackets, other sew-able items

______in abandoned piping or piping that looks connected but isn't actually connected and is fairly easily accessible. Pipes with caps on them, including piping accessible in basement.

______in the kitchen (food containers/freezer/fridge)

______sheds and all other outbuildings.

______search all cars on property thoroughly

______search all boxes, cans, containers in all out buildings.

______inside corners of any dirt floors

______check under the base/foot of hollowed out doors

______check out all removable top cans--paint, chemicals

______don't forget the doghouse and under-neath the doghouse in the back yard

______chicken coops too.

______check all water wells

______look for loose bricks all the way down to arms length.

______also look for loose bricks around the outside of the fireplace.

______look for depressions in the ground around and behind buildings and detect them.

MY SEARCHES

DATE:_______________________________________

ADDRESS:___________________________________

CITY_____________________________STATE________

WHAT DREW YOU TO THIS PLACE: __________

____

____

____

____

WHAT DID YOU FIND: _____________________

____

____

____

____

____

____

____

NOTES: ________________________

____

____

____

____

____

____

____

____

COMMENTS: ________________________

____

____

____

____

____

____

____

CHECK LIST
______air vents
______floor registers
______underneath all carpets
______false floor panels
______garden
______light fixtures
______loose legs on furniture
______inside piano bench
______figurines (stuffed inside)
______under window sills
______rolled up in socks
______inside books (also check for taped or stashed bills
______behind sleeve if book has one.)
______watch for book 'safes' where book is hollowed out in
   middle.
______shoes, be sure to check the toe area
______inside Speaker Cabinets
______inside toilet tank
______taped to bottom of toilet tank
______taped to the underneath sinks
______a hole in the wall covered with a poster.
______a hole in the wall under a stairway.
______taped to the top of a door.
______inside a smoke detector
______in the freezer
______in a box of Tampons (or any container under a sink)
______inside and underneath old sewing machines.
______check for false bottoms in trunks, tool boxes, toy-
   boxes, tackle boxes, etc.
______taped to the underneath bottom OR the back of
   hutches, china cabinets, tall dressers, buffets, etc..
______beds, mattress (Especially INSIDE the mattress.
   This is one of the most common places depression
   money was horded and later found.)
______look in their clothes and not just the pockets, they
   might have sewed something into the hems or virtually
   anywhere on the garment.
______on top of a suspended ceiling

______in attics

______inside of walls

______under false floors

______behind false walls (check closet walls too)

______behind all electrical outlets

______bottom of deep freeze

______underneath any runners on stairs, hallways and other places

______refrigerator inside container or Ziploc, even wrapped in white paper or foil like meat. etc.

______behind bricks in basement, floor of basement, old fireplaces.

______inside flower pots, look for Ziploc or other waterproof containers inside the soil.

______envelope taped behind the plumbing under sinks and behind toilets

______stitched into hems of curtains, jackets, other sew-able items

______in abandoned piping or piping that looks connected but isn't actually connected and is fairly easily accessible. Pipes with caps on them, including piping accessible in basement.

______in the kitchen (food containers/freezer/fridge)

______sheds and all other outbuildings.

______search all cars on property thoroughly

______search all boxes, cans, containers in all out buildings.

______inside corners of any dirt floors

______check under the base/foot of hollowed out doors

______check out all removable top cans--paint, chemicals

______don't forget the doghouse and under-neath the doghouse in the back yard

______chicken coops too.

______check all water wells

______look for loose bricks all the way down to arms length.

______also look for loose bricks around the outside of the fireplace.

______look for depressions in the ground around and behind buildings and detect them.

MY SEARCHES

DATE:____

ADDRESS:____

CITY___________________________STATE________

WHAT DREW YOU TO THIS PLACE: __________

____

____

____

____

WHAT DID YOU FIND: ______________________

____

____

____

____

____

____

____

____

NOTES: _______________________

____

____

____

____

____

____

____

____

COMMENTS: _______________________

____

____

____

____

____

____

CHECK LIST

______air vents

______floor registers

______underneath all carpets

______false floor panels

______garden

______light fixtures

______loose legs on furniture

______inside piano bench

______figurines (stuffed inside)

______under window sills

______rolled up in socks

______inside books (also check for taped or stashed bills behind sleeve if book has one.)

______watch for book 'safes' where book is hollowed out in middle.

______shoes, be sure to check the toe area

______inside Speaker Cabinets

______inside toilet tank

______taped to bottom of toilet tank

______taped to the underneath sinks

______a hole in the wall covered with a poster.

______a hole in the wall under a stairway.

______taped to the top of a door.

______inside a smoke detector

______in the freezer

______in a box of Tampons (or any container under a sink)

______inside and underneath old sewing machines.

______check for false bottoms in trunks, tool boxes, toyboxes, tackle boxes, etc.

______taped to the underneath bottom OR the back of hutches, china cabinets, tall dressers, buffets, etc..

______beds, mattress (Especially INSIDE the mattress. This is one of the most common places depression money was horded and later found.)

______look in their clothes and not just the pockets, they might have sewed something into the hems or virtually anywhere on the garment.

______on top of a suspended ceiling

______ in attics
______ inside of walls
______ under false floors
______ behind false walls (check closet walls too)
______ behind all electrical outlets
______ bottom of deep freeze
______ underneath any runners on stairs, hallways and other places
______ refrigerator inside container or Ziploc, even wrapped in white paper or foil like meat. etc.
______ behind bricks in basement, floor of basement, old fireplaces.
______ inside flower pots, look for Ziploc or other waterproof containers inside the soil.
______ envelope taped behind the plumbing under sinks and behind toilets
______ stitched into hems of curtains, jackets, other sew-able items
______ in abandoned piping or piping that looks connected but isn't actually connected and is fairly easily accessible. Pipes with caps on them, including piping accessible in basement.
______ in the kitchen (food containers/freezer/fridge)
______ sheds and all other outbuildings.
______ search all cars on property thoroughly
______ search all boxes, cans, containers in all out buildings.
______ inside corners of any dirt floors
______ check under the base/foot of hollowed out doors
______ check out all removable top cans--paint, chemicals
______ don't forget the doghouse and under-neath the doghouse in the back yard
______ chicken coops too.
______ check all water wells
______ look for loose bricks all the way down to arms length.
______ also look for loose bricks around the outside of the fireplace.
______ look for depressions in the ground around and behind buildings and detect them.

MY SEARCHES

DATE:_______________________________________

ADDRESS:_____________________________________

CITY_____________________________STATE________

WHAT DREW YOU TO THIS PLACE: __________

____

____

____

____

WHAT DID YOU FIND: _____________________

____

____

____

____

____

____

____

____

NOTES: ______________________

____

____

____

____

____

____

____

____

COMMENTS: ______________________

____

____

____

____

____

____

____

CHECK LIST

_______ air vents

_______ floor registers

_______ underneath all carpets

_______ false floor panels

_______ garden

_______ light fixtures

_______ loose legs on furniture

_______ inside piano bench

_______ figurines (stuffed inside)

_______ under window sills

_______ rolled up in socks

_______ inside books (also check for taped or stashed bills behind sleeve if book has one.)

_______ watch for book 'safes' where book is hollowed out in middle.

_______ shoes, be sure to check the toe area

_______ inside Speaker Cabinets

_______ inside toilet tank

_______ taped to bottom of toilet tank

_______ taped to the underneath sinks

_______ a hole in the wall covered with a poster.

_______ a hole in the wall under a stairway.

_______ taped to the top of a door.

_______ inside a smoke detector

_______ in the freezer

_______ in a box of Tampons (or any container under a sink)

_______ inside and underneath old sewing machines.

_______ check for false bottoms in trunks, tool boxes, toy-boxes, tackle boxes, etc.

_______ taped to the underneath bottom OR the back of hutches, china cabinets, tall dressers, buffets, etc..

_______ beds, mattress (Especially INSIDE the mattress. This is one of the most common places depression money was horded and later found.)

_______ look in their clothes and not just the pockets, they might have sewed something into the hems or virtually anywhere on the garment.

_______ on top of a suspended ceiling

______in attics
______inside of walls
______under false floors
______behind false walls (check closet walls too)
______behind all electrical outlets
______bottom of deep freeze
______underneath any runners on stairs, hallways and other places
______refrigerator inside container or Ziploc, even wrapped in white paper or foil like meat. etc.
______behind bricks in basement, floor of basement, old fireplaces.
______inside flower pots, look for Ziploc or other waterproof containers inside the soil.
______envelope taped behind the plumbing under sinks and behind toilets
______stitched into hems of curtains, jackets, other sew-able items
______in abandoned piping or piping that looks connected but isn't actually connected and is fairly easily accessible. Pipes with caps on them, including piping accessible in basement.
______in the kitchen (food containers/freezer/fridge)
______sheds and all other outbuildings.
______search all cars on property thoroughly
______search all boxes, cans, containers in all out buildings.
______inside corners of any dirt floors
______check under the base/foot of hollowed out doors
______check out all removable top cans--paint, chemicals
______don't forget the doghouse and under-neath the doghouse in the back yard
______chicken coops too.
______check all water wells
______look for loose bricks all the way down to arms length.
______also look for loose bricks around the outside of the fireplace.
______look for depressions in the ground around and behind buildings and detect them.

MY SEARCHES

DATE:_______________________________________

ADDRESS:____________________________________

CITY______________________________STATE_________

WHAT DREW YOU TO THIS PLACE: __________

____

____

____

____

WHAT DID YOU FIND: __________________

____

____

____

____

____

____

____

NOTES: _______________________________

____

____

____

____

____

____

____

____

____

COMMENTS: _______________________________

____

____

____

____

____

____

____

CHECK LIST
______air vents
______floor registers
______underneath all carpets
______false floor panels
______garden
______light fixtures
______loose legs on furniture
______inside piano bench
______figurines (stuffed inside)
______under window sills
______rolled up in socks
______inside books (also check for taped or stashed bills
______behind sleeve if book has one.)
______watch for book 'safes' where book is hollowed out in
   middle.
______shoes, be sure to check the toe area
______inside Speaker Cabinets
______inside toilet tank
______taped to bottom of toilet tank
______taped to the underneath sinks
______a hole in the wall covered with a poster.
______a hole in the wall under a stairway.
______taped to the top of a door.
______inside a smoke detector
______in the freezer
______in a box of Tampons (or any container under a sink)
______inside and underneath old sewing machines.
______check for false bottoms in trunks, tool boxes, toy-
   boxes, tackle boxes, etc.
______taped to the underneath bottom OR the back of
   hutches, china cabinets, tall dressers, buffets, etc..
______beds, mattress (Especially INSIDE the mattress.
   This is one of the most common places depression
   money was horded and later found.)
______look in their clothes and not just the pockets, they
   might have sewed something into the hems or virtually
   anywhere on the garment.
______on top of a suspended ceiling

______ in attics

______ inside of walls

______ under false floors

______ behind false walls (check closet walls too)

______ behind all electrical outlets

______ bottom of deep freeze

______ underneath any runners on stairs, hallways and other places

______ refrigerator inside container or Ziploc, even wrapped in white paper or foil like meat. etc.

______ behind bricks in basement, floor of basement, old fireplaces.

______ inside flower pots, look for Ziploc or other waterproof containers inside the soil.

______ envelope taped behind the plumbing under sinks and behind toilets

______ stitched into hems of curtains, jackets, other sew-able items

______ in abandoned piping or piping that looks connected but isn't actually connected and is fairly easily accessible. Pipes with caps on them, including piping accessible in basement.

______ in the kitchen (food containers/freezer/fridge)

______ sheds and all other outbuildings.

______ search all cars on property thoroughly

______ search all boxes, cans, containers in all out buildings.

______ inside corners of any dirt floors

______ check under the base/foot of hollowed out doors

______ check out all removable top cans--paint, chemicals

______ don't forget the doghouse and under-neath the doghouse in the back yard

______ chicken coops too.

______ check all water wells

______ look for loose bricks all the way down to arms length.

______ also look for loose bricks around the outside of the fireplace.

______ look for depressions in the ground around and *behind buildings and detect them.*

MY SEARCHES

DATE:_______________________________________

ADDRESS:_________________________________

CITY_______________________________STATE________

WHAT DREW YOU TO THIS PLACE: __________

____

____

____

____

WHAT DID YOU FIND: _____________________

____

____

____

____

____

____

____

NOTES: _________________________

COMMENTS: _______________________

CHECK LIST
_______air vents
_______floor registers
_______underneath all carpets
_______false floor panels
_______garden
_______light fixtures
_______loose legs on furniture
_______inside piano bench
_______figurines (stuffed inside)
_______under window sills
_______rolled up in socks
_______inside books (also check for taped or stashed bills
_______behind sleeve if book has one.)
_______watch for book 'safes' where book is hollowed out in
   middle.
_______shoes, be sure to check the toe area
_______inside Speaker Cabinets
_______inside toilet tank
_______taped to bottom of toilet tank
_______taped to the underneath sinks
_______a hole in the wall covered with a poster.
_______a hole in the wall under a stairway.
_______taped to the top of a door.
_______inside a smoke detector
_______in the freezer
_______in a box of Tampons (or any container under a sink)
_______inside and underneath old sewing machines.
_______check for false bottoms in trunks, tool boxes, toy-
   boxes, tackle boxes, etc.
_______taped to the underneath bottom OR the back of
   hutches, china cabinets, tall dressers, buffets, etc..
_______beds, mattress (Especially INSIDE the mattress.
   this is one of the most common places depression
   money was horded and later found.)
_______look in any clothes and not just the pockets, they
   might have sewed something into the hems or virtually
   anywhere on the garment.
_______on top of a suspended ceiling

______in attics
______inside of walls
______under false floors
______behind false walls (check closet walls too)
______behind all electrical outlets
______bottom of deep freeze
______underneath any runners on stairs, hallways and other places
______refrigerator inside container or Ziploc, even wrapped in white paper or foil like meat. etc.
______behind bricks in basement, floor of basement, old fireplaces.
______inside flower pots, look for Ziploc or other waterproof containers inside the soil.
______envelope taped behind the plumbing under sinks and behind toilets
______stitched into hems of curtains, jackets, other sew-able items
______in abandoned piping or piping that looks connected but isn't actually connected and is fairly easily accessible. Pipes with caps on them, including piping accessible in basement.
______in the kitchen (food containers/freezer/fridge)
______sheds and all other outbuildings.
______search all cars on property thoroughly
______search all boxes, cans, containers in all out buildings.
______inside corners of any dirt floors
______check under the base/foot of hollowed out doors
______check out all removable top cans--paint, chemicals
______don't forget the doghouse and under-neath the doghouse in the back yard
______chicken coops too.
______check all water wells
______look for loose bricks all the way down to arms length.
______also look for loose bricks around the outside of the fireplace.
______look for depressions in the ground around and behind buildings and detect them.

MY SEARCHES

DATE:______________________________________

ADDRESS:___________________________________

CITY______________________________STATE__________

WHAT DREW YOU TO THIS PLACE: ___________

____

____

____

____

WHAT DID YOU FIND: ___________________________

____

____

____

____

____

____

____

____

NOTES: _______________________________

____

____

____

____

____

____

____

____

COMMENTS: _______________________________

____

____

____

____

____

____

____

CHECK LIST

_____air vents
_____floor registers
_____underneath all carpets
_____false floor panels
_____garden
_____light fixtures
_____loose legs on furniture
_____inside piano bench
_____figurines (stuffed inside)
_____under window sills
_____rolled up in socks
_____inside books (also check for taped or stashed bills
_____behind sleeve if book has one.)
_____watch for book 'safes' where book is hollowed out in
   middle.
_____shoes, be sure to check the toe area
_____inside Speaker Cabinets
_____inside toilet tank
_____taped to bottom of toilet tank
_____taped to the underneath sinks
_____a hole in the wall covered with a poster.
_____a hole in the wall under a stairway.
_____taped to the top of a door.
_____inside a smoke detector
_____in the freezer
_____in a box of Tampons (or any container under a sink)
_____inside and underneath old sewing machines.
_____check for false bottoms in trunks, tool boxes, toy-
   boxes, tackle boxes, etc.
_____taped to the underneath bottom OR the back of
   hutches, china cabinets, tall dressers, buffets, etc..
_____beds, mattress (Especially INSIDE the mattress.
   this is one of the most common places depression
   money was horded and later found.)
_____look in their clothes and not just the pockets, they
   might have sewed something into the hems or virtually
   anywhere on the garment.
_____on top of a suspended ceiling

______in attics

______inside of walls

______under false floors

______behind false walls (check closet walls too)

______behind all electrical outlets

______bottom of deep freeze

______underneath any runners on stairs, hallways and other places

______refrigerator inside container or Ziploc, even wrapped in white paper or foil like meat. etc.

______behind bricks in basement, floor of basement, old fireplaces.

______inside flower pots, look for Ziploc or other waterproof containers inside the soil.

______envelope taped behind the plumbing under sinks and behind toilets

______stitched into hems of curtains, jackets, other sew-able items

______in abandoned piping or piping that looks connected but isn't actually connected and is fairly easily accessible. Pipes with caps on them, including piping accessible in basement.

______in the kitchen (food containers/freezer/fridge)

______sheds and all other outbuildings.

______search all cars on property thoroughly

______search all boxes, cans, containers in all out buildings.

______inside corners of any dirt floors

______check under the base/foot of hollowed out doors

______check out all removable top cans--paint, chemicals

______don't forget the doghouse and under-neath the doghouse in the back yard

______chicken coops too.

______check all water wells

______look for loose bricks all the way down to arms length.

______also look for loose bricks around the outside of the fireplace.

______look for depressions in the ground around and behind buildings and detect them.

MY SEARCHES

DATE:____

ADDRESS:______________________________________

CITY__________________________STATE_________

WHAT DREW YOU TO THIS PLACE: __________

____

____

____

____

WHAT DID YOU FIND: ____________________

____

____

____

____

____

____

NOTES: _______________________

____

____

____

____

____

____

____

COMMENTS: _______________________

____

____

____

____

____

____

CHECK LIST
______air vents
______floor registers
______underneath all carpets
______false floor panels
______garden
______light fixtures
______loose legs on furniture
______inside piano bench
______figurines (stuffed inside)
______under window sills
______rolled up in socks
______inside books (also check for taped or stashed bills
______behind sleeve if book has one.)
______watch for book 'safes' where book is hollowed out in
      middle.
______shoes, be sure to check the toe area
______inside Speaker Cabinets
______inside toilet tank
______taped to bottom of toilet tank
______taped to the underneath sinks
______a hole in the wall covered with a poster.
______a hole in the wall under a stairway.
______taped to the top of a door.
______inside a smoke detector
______in the freezer
______in a box of Tampons (or any container under a sink)
______inside and underneath old sewing machines.
______check for false bottoms in trunks, tool boxes, toy-
      boxes, tackle boxes, etc.
______taped to the underneath bottom OR the back of
      hutches, china cabinets, tall dressers, buffets, etc..
______beds, mattress (Especially INSIDE the mattress.
      This is one of the most common places depression
      money was horded and later found.)
______look in their clothes and not just the pockets, they
      might have sewed something into the hems or virtually
      anywhere on the garment.
______on top of a suspended ceiling

______ in attics
______ inside of walls
______ under false floors
______ behind false walls (check closet walls too)
______ behind all electrical outlets
______ bottom of deep freeze
______ underneath any runners on stairs, hallways and other places
______ refrigerator inside container or Ziploc, even wrapped in white paper or foil like meat. etc.
______ behind bricks in basement, floor of basement, old fireplaces.
______ inside flower pots, look for Ziploc or other waterproof containers inside the soil.
______ envelope taped behind the plumbing under sinks and behind toilets
______ stitched into hems of curtains, jackets, other sew-able items
______ in abandoned piping or piping that looks connected but isn't actually connected and is fairly easily accessible. Pipes with caps on them, including piping accessible in basement.
______ in the kitchen (food containers/freezer/fridge)
______ sheds and all other outbuildings.
______ search all cars on property thoroughly
______ search all boxes, cans, containers in all out buildings.
______ inside corners of any dirt floors
______ check under the base/foot of hollowed out doors
______ check out all removable top cans--paint, chemicals
______ don't forget the doghouse and under-neath the doghouse in the back yard
______ chicken coops too.
______ check all water wells
______ look for loose bricks all the way down to arms length.
______ also look for loose bricks around the outside of the fireplace.
______ look for depressions in the ground around and behind buildings and detect them.

If you enjoyed this book,
stop by and leave a review on
Amazon.
Just search for Auntie V.'s
in Amazon's search box on the top of every
Amazon page :)